Tony Robles will never forget the Hurricane Helene Flood, and we will never forget *Soup for the Storm*. Eulogistic of unlikely heroes, family, friends, and neighbors bonding amid the rusty dents of a trailer park, these poems recall the damaged and the spared with "a presence not even a hurricane can remove." Choosing contemplative darkness over restored power, Robles remembers other catastrophes, such as Katrina and Gaza, when his being becomes "an intersection between here and there," enabling us to see our own experiences with more light through these necessary poems.

—Hilda Downer, poet and editor of *Had I a Dove: Appalachian Poets on the Helene Flood*

In *Soup for the Storm*, Tony Robles brings a singular voice to literature shaped by catastrophe. This sequence of poems centers on trailer park residents who survived Hurricane Helene, rendering their efforts to hold onto ordinary life amid ruin. Through intimate portraits and layered backstories tracing their journeys from far-flung places to the mountains of Western North Carolina, the poems reveal how, in the long wait for electricity to return, these survivors come to recognize a deeper, more sustaining power: community.

—Tim Peeler, author and poet of *Trap Game*

Tony Robles' *Soup for the Storm: Poems of Hurricane Helene*, a product of his ground-zero experience with the hurricane and written in the hours and weeks following, is a thick, simmering stew of poems chock-full of heartfelt emotions, reflections, and self-discovery. This important work is not only a historical poetic record of the event, but the words contained within also serve as a common cathartic voice for the thousands affected by Helene, and will no doubt facilitate introspection and healing for many years to come.

—Suzette Clark Bradshaw, North Carolina poet and Helene survivor

Soup for the Storm

Poems of Hurricane Helene

TONY ROBLES

REDHAWK PUBLICATIONS

Soup for the Storm Poems of Hurricane Helene

ISBN: 979-8-89933-019-3 (Paperback)
Library of Congress Control Number: 2026904536

Cover Design: Erin M. Mann
Book Design: Amber Zezeck

Printed in the United States of America.
First printing 2026.

Redhawk Publications
The Catawba Valley Community College Press
2550 Hwy 70 SE
Hickory, NC 28602

https://redhawkpublications.com

This project was supported by ArtsAVL, Bank of America, and the North Carolina Arts Council, a division of the Department of Natural and Cultural Resources.

For Mom and Pete

Also by the Author

Lakas and the Manilatown Fish
(Children's Book Press, 2003)

Lakas and the Makibaka Hotel
(Lee & Low Books, 2006)

BORN N' RAISED IN FRISCO: Words, Art and Resistance from a Colonized Displaced City Vol. 1

Cool Don't Live Here No More—A Letter to San Francisco

Fingerprints of a Hunger Strike

Thrift Store Metamorphasis
(Redhawk Publications, 2023)

Where the Warehouse Things Are
(Redhawk Publications, 2024)

"There is peace even in the storm."

–Vincent Van Gogh

Table of Contents

Introduction: Helene, a Name I Refuse to Forget

It is Monday, October 7, 2024. Hurricane Helene ran wild in this part of North Carolina. Nobody saw it coming. We knew a big storm was heading our way but we thought that Florida would get the lion's share, the brunt of it. But Helene traveled upwards through Georgia, South Carolina, North Carolina, and into Tennessee, leaving in its wake a landscape torn asunder. Western North Carolina, the place I have lived for five and a half years, relocating from San Francisco to be closer to my mother who lives in Bat Cave. I've lived in Hendersonville, a small town about 20 minutes or so from Asheville, a city known for its art scene; sometimes referred to as the "Berkeley of the South." There are Bay Area expats there as well, those who came to Western North Carolina for the mountains, the allure of the climate, to escape an insane rental market, gentrification, etc.

We collectively thought that while destructive hurricanes hit the coast—known as the Outer Banks—their remnants dispersed and dissipated towards the mountainous west, bringing havoc but much less severe. We'd received alerts from the National Weather Service warning of major flooding—life-threatening flooding—upon the arrival of Helene. We were not told to evacuate. The hurricane hit our area on Thursday. I woke at 4:30 a.m. to the sound of howling wind and trees and branches shaking and snapping. Thirty minutes later I heard a scream.

I looked out my window. A large tree had been uprooted and had fallen on a nearby unit in our mobile home park. I watched from my bedroom.

I thought about my mother in the mountains in Bat Cave, a short distance from Lake Lure and Chimney Rock, severely damaged places now burned into memory. In the case of Chimney Rock, a quaint tourist town, its total destruction. Same fate for Lake Lure, known as the location for the movie Dirty Dancing. Both places are within a short distance from one another, with my mother in the mountains in nearby Bat Cave. We had no power, no cell service, no internet, conveniences I realized I took for granted. Markets were thankfully open but only accepted cash. I got a call from my mother in spite of the spotty cell phone service. She said she was being airlifted from her home in the mountains. Her house wasn't damaged, she said, but everything else was—roads, bridges—all points of entrance and exit swept away in the torrent. My mom bid me goodbye. I could hear the helicopter over the phone. She and my stepfather were flown to North Hendersonville High School and from there driven to my stepfather's brother's house. I reunited with them later in the evening.

Days went by, ten without power, several without water. My mobile home community, Summerpath Village, rallied together. One resident had a generator. The property had a clubhouse where we gathered, talked, and strategized on how to get by without electricity, what food was available, how to get water, and other essentials. The clubhouse was a hub. Some had lost their homes, including a woman in her 80s who had significant health problems. Fortunately, she was pulled from her home, unharmed but shaken; a large tree had fallen on her unit and crushed it.

"When's the power coming back?" we all asked. We'd heard it would be a week, then more than a week. Water had been restored, but we were advised to boil it due to the damage done to water treatment facilities and possible damage to pipes. But we couldn't boil it because we didn't have electricity. Our mobile home community's residents were in disbelief that it had hit our area. Some had experienced hurricanes; one resident had lived through three of them in Florida.

In the weeks prior to Helene, we'd had heavy rainfall. The ground had been saturated by rainfall. The energy caused by a warm front, wind, and rain was sustained and did not dissipate. This caused mudslides that devastated mountainous regions, valleys, and hollows (known across Appalachia as "hollers."). Homes were swept away in places like Swannanoa, an area with many trailer homes that sustained tremendous damage. Other areas like Boone, Nebo, Waynesville, and Bakersville sustained extreme damage as well.

In the aftermath of Helene, we waited for power to be restored. It was restored yesterday, a little after 10 a.m. As the electricity came back, the clicks and knocks and pings of devices came out of hibernation. It seemed that a sense of normalcy was quickly reclaiming what had been taken away days prior. It seemed that normalcy was sneaking in too quickly. I write this by candlelight. I have not turned on the lights in my mobile home unit. I don't want to forget what happened here. I don't want to take the light for granted. I don't want to forget what was taken from us temporarily by Helene. Many others lost far more than we did. We must remember.

(Reprinted from Positively Filipino Magazine, October 9, 2024)

Visitor

The water claimed the
Shape of our bodies

Took possession of our eyes

Shook everything
In its path

Trees wept
Before the fall

Supine in time's
Sudden suspension

Scattered
Burning leaves of
Silence

A story uncovered

Fleeing into itself

As the landscape lingered

In Helene's silent rage

Airlift (For my mother)

The sound of chopper blades
comes through the phone

Connection severed

Her voice cuts
Through the frenzy

We're being airlifted, she says

A military helicopter

No time to pack

A bang on the door:
Time to evacuate!

She and her husband
Gather a few meager belongings
Before negotiating the ravine's
of a muddy slope

The stepfather, a big man
Was nearly swallowed by the ravine's
Ravenous mudfish mouth filled with
dead flowers and mournful hymns

The mother
Severed
Separated from her home

Her colorful soaps
In dishes the shape
Of antique bathtubs
the tint of bath salts

And a guitar she lifts and
nestles to her body that now
Tilts against her shadow

Held hostage by a house
Deprived of her presence

I think of the mother
Lifted into the air as a baby
By her mother, her father

The sound of her weeping
And cooing like the stings of
guitars

Sitting silent in
Her mountain home

Awaiting her return

Helene

I don't want to forget how you
rattled trees, shook me awake
At 4:30 a.m.
I don't want to forget the
Community stripped of power
But in coming together
Realizing we have power

I don't want to forget
Manang Francisca in the Supermarket,
The only Filipino face I saw, walking
Aimlessly with a gallon of milk in one
Hand and a rosary in the other as if
Balancing the scales of have and have not

Manang! Manang! I cried out
Stand in line with me!

The line was a looping embrace
Holding whatever our arms could claim

A Circumference of people
told that it was cash only
after standing in line for
15 min....30 min

Manang Francisca and I waited
In line together for nearly two
Hours but it seemed like a lifetime
As she told me that her grandma had
Lived through the war with the Spanish

I don't want to forget groping in the dark,
Fingers traced the amplitude of their uncertainty
Neighbors whose faces I finally saw in
The darkness, a darkness so clear as my
Fingers felt every dip and curve and contour

I don't want to forget the neighbor
Who argued with his Chihuahua, Norman,
Every morning, bickering, saying: Damn
It, Norman! I don't have time for your
Bullshit!

I don't want to forget the fallen
Trees and the roots exposed
To both darkness and light

I don't want to forget my
Neighbor Jorge Luis Vasquez Colon
Who helped clear the snapped limbs
Of trees with his own limbs tattooed with
the wailing songs of Taino ancestors

Boricua! Boricua!

I don't want to forget
Manong Gio in Edneyville who
Had no power, no water

I don't want to forget
Bringing him a canister of water
Tubig! He cried out

I don't want to forget the dark
Because it is in the darkness that I
Drank bits of precious light

I don't want to forget my
Mother telling me to hunker down
And the pounding sound
Of wind and rain on the stained
Drum skin of my heart
As all fades to black

I don't want to
Forget what happened here
As I write this
In the light of a candle
The day after the power
Came back

Manang: A Filipino term of respect for an older Filipino woman.
Manong; A term of respect for an older Filipino man.
Tubig: The Filipino word for water

Seedling

Removing a lemon seed
From yellow flesh,
I remember

The hurricane
Knocking over trees
In this mobile home park

Houses
Pummeled

Including the home of
A woman in her
Late 80's

She was pulled from her
Home in the aftermath

The wind howled as it
Pulled trees by the roots

Toppling
Homes

With their fragile
Walls, screen doors

Where we once
Got a glimpse of the
Old woman preserving
Green beans in a mason jar

All that remains of
Her home is branches and
Dirt

And a poet
Who is thankful his
Home survived

Who will plant a lemon
Seedling in remembrance
On her plot of land

Without bitterness

Just a memory
Preserved

4 Trees

Herman told me that
All great powers fall

Countries
Dictators

He would take a swig of wine
As his words swirled
Into my young mind

He'd screw the
Cap back onto the bottle
Which sometimes held wisdom
Which often fell to the
Floor

And close his eyes

Months after the hurricane
I look out the window at
4 large trees, two on either side
Of my mobile home

And how its branches fall on
The roof sounding like
Small explosions

And squirrels scurry across
Leaving a trail of sounds seeking
an ear's hollow sanctuary
I remember Herman's words

All great powers fall

But these 4 trees
Didn't fall

Didn't crush my
Home

Thank the trees
And their silent power

And Herman for
Propping them up

Robert's Turkey Soup
Days after Hurricane Helene

In this mobile home community in
Hendersonville, North Carolina
Resides someone who'd be described
As the local oddball

A downward splash of brown hair
Falls on his forehead and he is often
Seen bare-chested when it's sunny
Carrying his contribution to nature's
Symphony: A gas-powered leaf blower

You see him one day
And he waves and smiles

The next day he acts like
He hadn't seen you the day
Before

The local oddball took offense
To Hurricane Helene

Who does she think she is
Trying to out oddball
Me? He said

And the trees were uprooted
And fell on homes and
The wind howled and the odd
Ball rolled up his sleeves and lifted
A tree trunk from that old woman's
Mobile home and pulled her out

He's everywhere, now

hauling
moving
Cutting fallen trees
With a chainsaw

Tonight he hovers near a propane
Stove stirring something thick
In a pot

He ladles some into a cup
And hands it to me

It's turkey soup,
The oddball said

I tasted it,
It is thick, it is like
No other soup I'd ever tasted

I put rice and oatmeal to
Thicken it, he said

The stars overhead stop
Stirring and ask, who's
That oddball

I look up and say,
His name is Robert

I think of oddballs in other
communities
Across the state who didn't make
it

As Robert's thick turkey soup
Unstills the palette

Adam in the Mountains of Bat Cave

A tongue of
Mountain earth

A bed of weeds

Teeth stained with honey
And blossoms

A beard filled with moss

A body tainted with hope,
Curiosity

In the cave of his mind are
Equations carved on earthen
Walls

Always within earshot of
When the wind beckons

The handiest of men

Entrusted to patch roofs
With pieces of sky and resuscitate

Windows with the breath of
Intuition

With hands that bend
Lightning into useful tools
Adam, who says that weeds
Sprouting from the ground are
“rising up through the opposition.”

Adam who rose when Helene came
Helping his neighbors
Off the mountain until he was
The only one left

All roads blocked
He faced the opposition of wind,
Rain and the thrashing of branches
Against his skin

With no way out
Except through the dark cave
Of lingering quandaries

With stained fingers
He inscribes on its wall
The only equation he needs

His touch

Feeling his way
Through the rocks, the weeds
Cutting into the muddy clarity of a
River

Sliding off
The mountain
Only to return

Non-Perishable

The line at the supermarket
Was a loop with me at the tail end

The shelf had one case of water left
That leapt into my arms with
a lover's dispossessed passion

(Does mere desire hold water?)

It's cash only, we are told by a
Muffled voice overhead as the machines
We count on are trapped behind
Barcodes of silence

In line with a hundred or more
People ahead of me

Legions of eyes, limbs,
Torsos, noses and muted
Debit cards

All lined up not knowing what lie
Ahead

I had cash at home, a short
Distance away

Can you hold my spot, I asked
The middle aged couple in
Front of me

Yeah, sure

I lay my water down
And rushed home, driving past
An old resident of the mobile home
Park who always waves, smiles,
Gives the thumbs up sign

I sped past him with my
Printed currency and resumed my spot
In the supermarket line

As the line inched forward
non-perishables found
Their way into my hands: Peanut
Butter, pork rinds

I pay for my items, grateful
To have gotten them

I weave past downed power
Lines, fallen trees, crushed homes
Towards the old man as I inch my
Way back home

He gives me a wave,
A smile, a thumbs-up

Things
Non-perishable

Repair

The wind tore through
The mobile home

Left a gaping
Hole on the front end

Where
The silence of ten thousand
Sparrows spewed forth
Calloused shadows
Of father and son

Testing
The patience of skies
And the incessant sound of rusted
Hinges

Patching the hole with
Beer cans swollen with
Froth and hissing innards
Of muted words

An open wound flower
of endless sky

And remnants of a
Hurricane

Leaving father
And son

With things
To repair

Island People (For Petson)

There are island people
In this mountain town

They weave through
Currents and curves, navigating every
Twist of road

And thought

Island people from Micronesia

Creating islands
With their hands

Islands of generosity
In a womb of

Humility
Silence

Sharing roast pig,
Rice and taro and the gift
Of their music carved into
The mountains

The Island People travelled
The twisting path of the mountains
Navigating as their ancestors did
Across seas
leaving behind songs and poetry
in the skin of trees and the hues
of 10,000 jagged flowers

Songs and poetry that
Helene could not silence

One of the island people
Is a man with an island smile
Carved into the mountains of
Western North Carolina

A man whose family was in
Need of water after the hurricane

A man I had worked with
In the passing breath of a
season

I went to his home
with several jugs of water

He opened the door

I see his face
For the first time,
again

A face whose eyes carry words
Of water across islands and
Time zones and barriers into
The mountains

Eyes that carry
Water I thirst for

A Few Nights after Hurricane Helene

I write this poem
By candlelight

2 flickers of
Flame in a dance
On the heated wax
Of a scented candle

Giving off a glow
Of amber

Just yesterday my mom and stepfather
Were airlifted from their home in the
mountains

A home of plants and lamps and
Rugs and lights and globes that held
The world in their living room

The house wasn't damaged
But most of the surrounding area
was

Roads, bridges, trails
Discarded by a pillage of
rainwater and wind

They can't go
Back, not now

But they recently
Celebrated their 54th
Wedding anniversary

Two flickering lights
Giving off love's flame

In spite of
hurricanes
wars
disasters

Their love is their
home
Giving off a glow

Allowing me just enough
Light to write the end
Of this poem with the simple
Words: Mom and Pete, I love
you

Power (After Hurricane Helene)

We have no power
We have no lights
We have darkness
and stars and crickets
and splinters that have
pierced our roads and the
skin of our homes and our eyes

We grope about
looking for a candle
to guide the lost light
of our eyes

Searching for
the doorknob, the
keyhole

Perhaps the light is there

We have no power
But I've met
neighbors here that I've
never spoken to

And in the calmness of
night, I see the light in
their eyes

As they see the light
in mine

And we realize
somehow
we have
power

Po' Boy

Bobby has a sunburnt
Smile and skin that has
Simmered under the Louisiana
Sun

Fled New Orleans
After Katrina

Delivers wheelchairs and
Commodes and hospital
Beds to those who cannot
Flee

Tobacco burns his
Tongue as he spits a string
Of brown phlegm
Out the window

It hits the ground and
Sizzles like pieces of
regret

Speaks of little league
Dreams and a father
In the distance

With nothing but
Grass between them that
He cut over and over again

He can't flee the
Silence between them

Helene visited and created
A wide empty space
Around his home

Fallen trees
And flooding

Wide spaces between
He and his neighbors

Which he closes by
Offering the splintered
Song of his hands

As he spits out
Another wad of tobacco

Swannanoa

The sound of it
Slides off the tongue

The thought leaves a bite mark

Where the brown water and mud
Made its way onto skin

Sliding into a place

Quiet with splinters

Its kindling
a sibilance of water's rage

In the endless
Throat

Of night

Bakersville

Remember passing through

A small town

A post office
And few buildings

A restaurant with
Few tables

A red and white
Checked table cloth

Salt and pepper shakers
That could tell by the lift
And drop of the wrist if you
Were from here or from there

The waitress wiped the
Table cloth clean

Granules fell
Somewhere

And Helene came

Whose hand wiped
Across roads, streets, buildings
And into memory

A small town I'd have forgotten
If not for a girl

A coworker who was born
And raised there

Whose hands gathered clothes,
Blankets, food and love to send
Back home on a pallet of scuff
Marks and splinters

Hieroglyphics of the
Heart's deep chambers

En route to a place called Bakersville

A place I'd visited once

Whose restaurant had
Salt and pepper shakers and
A red and white checked
Table cloth

Coffin

On TV we saw
It

A coffin tumbling
Downward in a nature's
cruel gamble

Inside

A shard of moon seeking
Refuge

dust

a misshapen whisper

a song seeking voice

In a procession of
Leaves, branches

Bloated bodies in
Motion

Becoming one with
Water

As the memory of
Helene
Left its stinging
Song

In our eyes

Map

A year after Hurricane
Helene

I stop and look at a map
Of North Carolina posted
On the workplace wall

Lines and curves
Of interstates and roads

The names of towns,
Small and large

Some I've visited,
Most I never will

After the hurricane
My neighbors sat in the
Clubhouse of the mobile
Home park

A coming together
Of folks from north, south,
East, west

An atlas of bones,
Tendons and flesh with tendencies
To ache

Holding conversations
Or nodding off in a
in the grip of words unshapen

Some sit with legs
Exposed, ankles

Varicose veins
Crisscrossing a map
Of skin

Evidence
Of roads damaged,
Repaired

Travelled

Summerpath Storm

The path of the storm
Like a snake
Swirls ahead towards
Jorge Luis Vasquez Colon who
Lives in this mobile home
Park in Hendersonville, North Carolina

He says that the Spanish
Word for snake is Culebra

And it twists my tongue as
I repeat it

Born in Ponce, Puerto Rico
Grew up in Brooklyn
Finds himself living with
His French bulldog Ravi in a
Trailer

Has music in his blood
His muscle
His bone

His heart collects the beating breath
Of the Conga
And the Bongo

Taino ancestors are
Tattoed on the four corners
Of his body

His eyes capture wind

From under
His cap with the Borinquen
Flag stitched in
He reveals his musical
Instruments, first the bongo

BonGO! He says, correcting
My pronunciation: BONgo

He takes up arms against
The storm that has come

His arsenal: Conga drums,
A Wooden instrument with seeds
That makes rain sounds along with
The kalimba and maracas and other
Things that make sounds that can
Heal trees and make the wind
Whisper

With the music of his limbs
He pulls the branches of trees
That have been torn from their
trunks

He assumes our limbs as his own,
Lifting us into an unbreakable
embrace in this community
Of mobile homes called
Summerpath village

As we work together to
Mend, heal, rebuild
In a place called
Hendersonville

Over Here, Over There
(After Hurricane Helene)

Writing this at 422 Am
fortunate to have a bit of
light while others wade in
murky waters of muted darkness

Who can sleep?

Floating in uncertainty
threadbare fingers stitching prayers

The 4 trees surrounding my mobile
home in Hendersonville, NC decided
not to bend or snap or completely
uproot themselves during the
Hurricane

Decided not to
succumb to gravity and
assume a horizontal nature

Hurricanes and disasters
have always taken place "Over There"

They had names
that lie innocuous on the tongue from
afar:
Katrina
Ian
Harvey
Maria
and dozens more

I'd watch the images of destruction
on an electronic box and feel bad
for a moment

I'd even donate a few
dollars to charity before
resuming my regularly scheduled
activities

But "Over There" is
now "Over Here"

And people have died
and cities have washed away
and roads and bridges have collapsed
in the wind and rain and release of
river's rage

and in a small clubhouse at the mobile
home park where I live, we are fortunate
to have a generator
and a TV that residents gather in front
of to gather info on the destruction leveled
by Helene

The picture cuts to
another image

The destruction in a place called Gaza

over there

on the screen in front of us

In the Dark
(After Hurricane Helene)

The power came back
2 weeks ago

yet
I sit in the dark

Power line workers
came from other states
working long hours
to ensure we have
lights

and electricity to run
those things that run
us

I am powerless to
turn on the light

It's too easy
To turn on the
light and not see anything

I sit in the dark
not wanting to
forget

My neighbors,
the shapes of their faces,
their fears, their sadness,
stoicism
faith

With only the moon
and a sprinkle of stars
to illuminate the constellations
that separate us

I don't want to
forget the force fed
darkness that fed my
belly with gratitude

I don't want to
turn the lights on
just yet

lest I forget

What it was like
to finally see

Soup for the Storm

My mother fought
The mountain she once
Flocked to

Had planted
A garden

And scattered
Seeds of songs
That she hummed in the
Patience of sky and rain

She pulled herself from
The mountain in
Helene's wake

As the roots took a hold
Of her

Pulling her towards
The earth

She and her husband
Pulled themselves over mud
And branches and ditches

And into a military helicopter

And landed at her
Brother in law's home

A barricade of
brick

Where my hands break
Through walls of silence

Penetrating a cupboard
In search of
A pinch of gratitude
A dash of grace
Faith

love

to prepare a pot of chicken soup

Pulling my mother close

Hurricane Hero, a Guy Named Red

All I know is that
his name is Red
and that Red
drives an American
built pick-up truck with
bumper stickers in the rear
one of which says,
tourist season is here,
why can't we shoot them?

Another sticker appears to
have the image of an Elk
screwing a buffalo from
behind

(Not being a follower of
nature programs, I could be
wrong)

And Red happened to arrive
a few minutes after I'd plowed
my small rusted 2 door car
with 275,000 miles into a
small ditch

tried to move it
nothing but spinning wheels
and the cylindrical spittle of dirt

A lapse in concentration trying
to go from point A-Z, checking
on my mother after the hurricane
and worrying about things I
wouldn't worry about under normal
conditions

Red pulled up, looked at my car
that was halfway in the ditch
with the right rear tire in the air

He bent down and looked
underneath

I can hook my chain
under there and pull it
out, Red said

and I got into my car,
took a hold of the wheel,
put it in gear

Red pulled my car as if
pulling a glorious chunk
of gold or a rusted tooth

I was out of the ditch
Pulled out by
a man in a pick-up with a few dents and very
interesting bumper stickers

A guy I'd probably never
talk to under normal
circumstances

A guy with Red hair and
a red beard
whose name
is Red

Seeds

Driving down the highway
before coming to an
intersection

an intersection between
here and there
near and miss

A pick up truck in front
has a sticker emblazoned
on its rear window

The image of an assault rifle
with the words, one shot,
one kill displayed underneath
the words:"We the people"

The light turns green
and we move in opposite
directions

Not long ago a hurricane swept
through this area leaving behind
its riddles of tragedy

Its memory moves through my
body as I make my way towards
a store to pick up seeds

a new season
approaching

I will plant
many seeds
or
perhaps just one

I will surrender my hands
to earth's patient womb
of thistles and thorns

a reminder that I am of
the earth and that the earth
will one day reclaim me

One sun
One season
One intersection

Linemen after Hurricane Helene

Linemen

Electrical Workers

Driving in from other states

Fixing downed power lines
Mangled, severed
Removing fallen trees

Linemen, in the crossfire
doing what needs to be done

How many miles of power lines
have I driven past, walked past
without noticing?

I once saw a squirrel
run across a power line
along the Greenville Highway

jolts of agility and balance
in their tails

The linemen possess
their own ingenuity
and balance

After the hurricane
we were numb with the lack
of power, our digits unaccustomed
to clicking and hitting switches with
no response

No lights

and we saw the linemen
pouring in one by one in
trucks with in state and out
of state license plates
fixing, repairing

Even the squirrels were
dumbfounded

And on various power poles
you'll find signs that
read: Jesus Saves and
God Loves you

Many people can quote
the Bible every which way
in this corner of the world

including:
and God said, let
there be light
and there was light

lineman pour
in from everywhere

while squirrels wait to
scurry across wires

Next Door Neighbor after Hurricane Helene

He'd been my neighbor
in this mobile home park
for 5 years

Never talked to him
or if I did, it was in the form
of a cursory nod or quick glance

being the only non-white person
in this mobile home community
(Well, that's changed in the last
year), I had been cautious

In the days after Hurricane Helene
I saw him walking, carrying a
portable oxygen tank

tubes forced into
nostrils

I have COPD, he says
And we sat together in a makeshift
gathering area outdoors where food
and water and stories were
shared

stretching all to the last bite,
the last word as if it could be

His name is Roland
And the oxygen enters
his lungs through tubes,
each breath a reminder
a blessing

I told him that, incidentally,
I worked for a nearby
business that provides
portable oxygen machines

that we could possibly
help him

He thought that was a good
Idea

In the aftermath of
the hurricane
it was nice to finally
meet my next door
neighbor

it was like a
burst of fresh air

Demolition

She'd survived a
Stoke and
Her home survived
The hurricane

A home of
Dents and riddles and
Blemishes

Withstanding threats of
Demolition from the out of
State property owner

She would drive past my
House and wave from
The window

The rust and blemishes from
Her car would shed like petals from
A windblown flower

The dents seemed
To mend themselves

During the hurricane she
Revealed that she had once
Taught at a religious school
In Central America

I thought she was a
Mere woman with a rusted
Home riddled with dents and
A car with too many miles
And one day
I looked out my window
And saw her home devoured
By the steel jaws of an excavator

A bare space now
Occupies what was once
Her home

A woman with a smile that
Rust and dents could not
Remove

Not even a
hurricane

a story
To excavate

Jose (For Jose Case)

He stood in line at
The supermarket the day
After Hurricane Helene

Assuming his place in his
Hometown among many
Newcomers, transplants
And those firmly rooted

Hands reaching into shelves
Clutching at this or that with
Hands holding perishable and
Non-perishable measures
of accountability

And Jose watches
From his place in line
with the people among him,
Unaware that he is a weatherman

Having weathered every
Storm

A conduit of wind
And rain and flood who knows
The temperature on the surface
And below the skin of his hometown

A weathervane in his blood
Holds court with
The elements

His weapons

A stuffed toy bird
A harmonica
A guitar with broken strings
A cowboy hat

Firmly rooted to the ground
In Hendersonville

Waving at passing cars
On Main Street and along
The Spartanburg Highway

Jose whose arms and legs
And mind move in a dance
Of wind

Conducting a hometown symphony
Of comings and goings

A presence not
Even a hurricane can remove

Canadians During Hurricane Helene

Steve with the thick
southern accent and sun baked
curvature of cheek and jaw
traced in parchment from the
map of his life in Western
North Carolina

After Hurricane Helene
he told us he saw someone
stealing copper from a downed
power line

He yelled at the guy with a throat
thick with bird feathers and the guy
ran holding the copper as if it were
a serpent

Steve, with the southern accent
thicker than copper wire, an easy
tongue that can still a serpent

Says that electrical workers from
Canada descended on his block
to repair poles and wires

He detected an accent in their
voices and asked, where y'all from?
Canada they replied

Those Canadians were something,
Steve said. Took 'em 2 days to snap
those poles into shape

Those guys were something else

Steve, the guy with the thick
southern accent and a crew of
Canadians with accents

The crew was gone
when the work was done
leaving Steve with an urge to
wet his throat's feathers with
Canadian beer

Leaving their work and their
accents in Steve's ears

Steve, the guy with vocal
chords that awaken flocks
of Canada geese

leading them towards
the Blue Ridge Mountains

Landing on wires
Sharing their accented
Songs across Western North
Carolina

Manong Giordani Acu
2 weeks after Hurricane Helene

Manong Gio sits in his
silver car in the parking lot
of the supermarket where he
works part time

works the cash register in
the deli department, sitting on a
stool like a boxer in the late rounds
of a fight

His 73 year old legs
Going into the late rounds

Gio, Gio! the customers say
as they pay for their food,
engaging in nuggets of small
talk

exchanging observations
about the weather, cars, the price
of gas and life's unseen patterns

Do these people know that
the manong is a philosopher?

He has lived past lives:
A samurai warrior
in feudal Japan
An explorer who foraged
into the flesh of foreign lands

As well as a member of the
Cherokee nation before the
US was even a country

Manong Gio waits for me
in his car and I arrive

We talk about the hurricane
that hit a couple weeks back

His house survived unscathed
but nearby roads collapsed
under the falling gavel of trees

We sit in the car and
look at the trees whose leaves
breach the limits of our eyes

I tell him of a garden I
planted this season

Nothing grew, I say
As the colors of trees
invade our eyes

You must respect the trees,
manong Gio says
They give you shade, fruit
...paper too

We sit and the colors and contours
of Manong Gio's words stain
the sheafs of my mind where seeds
of poems are planted

a garden where nothing grows
but our friendship

Stars after Helene

The hurricane hit 5
days ago

we had no water
no power

Helene, we didn't see
you coming

we didn't think you'd
stir things up the way
you did

Lives washed
past with the
current

we blinked and
things were different

We didn't recognize
those places that
were so recognizable

But drops of water
continue to drop from
branches

Words formed from drops
of rain from storm's misshapen
tongue
words that awaken the heart's
broken music box

"How are you, brother, sister?
Do you have food, power, anything?

I lost my house
I lost my...
But thank God
we got our lives,
everything else can be
replaced

At night I walk around
the mobile home park where
I live

Houses have been destroyed,
huge trees uprooted

Painful splinters
ignited by the night sky

Night has fallen
and I look at the stars
of a night in Western North
Carolina

I never looked at them
before

They look down and
I look up at them
for the first time

They're beautiful

Acknowledgments

Thanks to the North Carolina Arts Council for funding this project. Thanks to editor Patty Thompson and Redhawk Publications for their encouragement and support. Special thanks to those who donated to my mother and stepfather's GoFundMe campaign in Helene's aftermath. Much appreciation to my friend, writer David Cameron for his keen eye and invaluable feedback. Thank you to Payton Grant for reading with a sensitive eye. Gratitude to my neighbors in Hendersonville who showed me what true community looks like. Thanks to Beverly Parayno, Christina and Stacey Olague, Paul Mayberry, Calvin Avery, Adam Newby, Jorge Luis Vasquez Colon, Manong Giordani Ocu, Petson Tihpen, Jose Case, Suzi Leonard and my spiritual family at Agape World Outreach. Love and remembrance to the late Kathleen Fox and Jimmy Huntley of Bat Cave, North Carolina.

About the Author

Tony Robles is the author of the poetry collections, *Cool Don't Live Here No More—A Letter to San Francisco, Fingerprints of a Hunger Strike, Thrift Store Metamorphosis* and *Where the Warehouse Things Are.* He was named Carl Sandburg Writer in Residence by the Friends of Carl Sandburg in Flat Rock, NC, in 2020. He was short-listed for Poet Laureate of San Francisco in 2017. His poetry, short stories, and essays have appeared in numerous publications. He earned his MFA in creative writing from Vermont College of Fine Arts in 2023 and is currently a professor of creative writing in the MFA graduate program at Lenoir Rhyne University in North Carolina.

www.ingramcontent.com/pod-product-compliance
Lightning Source LLC
LaVergne TN
LVHW010630100826
845148LV00014B/3178

* 9 7 9 8 8 9 9 3 3 0 1 9 3 *